IF YOU CAN WALK
YOU CAN SKI

IF YOU CAN WALK YOU CAN SKI

FRANK DAY

ILLUSTRATED BY ED VEBELL

SPECIAL CHILDREN'S SECTION

BY ANN DAY

COLLIER BOOKS

A DIVISION OF MACMILLAN PUBLISHING CO., INC.
New York
COLLIER MACMILLAN PUBLISHERS
London

*This book is dedicated to all
my students—past, present and future*

Library of Congress Catalog Card Number: 63-7966

GV
854
.D3
1962

FIRST COLLIER BOOKS EDITION 1967

THIRD PRINTING 1973

If You can Walk You Can Ski was originally published in a hardcover
edition by The Crowell-Collier Press
Macmillan Publishing Co., Inc.
866 Third Avenue, New York, N.Y. 10022
Collier-Macmillan Canada Ltd., Toronto, Canada

Printed in the United States of America

ACKNOWLEDGMENTS

I would like to thank Allen Weeden, Mr. and Mrs. Boris Todrin and
Kenneth Winters for their editorial assistance; Roland Palmedo for his
valuable suggestions and *Skiing: The International Sport,* which he
edited, as well as the many skiers who have stayed at Knoll Farm Inn
during the last two winters that read the manuscript and made suggestions.

I would also like to express my deepest appreciation to Mr. George
M. Kendall, director of the MacDowell Colony, Peterborough, who
advised me to become a ski instructor; the late Hannes Schneider,
who encouraged and inspired me; Bob Johnson, owner and operator
of the Newton, Mass. Indoor Ski School; and Weston Blake, whose
constant efforts for safer ski areas have been a source of inspiration.

I would also like to thank Pat O'Connor and Ruth Wolfert for their
creative editing.

Contents

IF YOU CAN WALK
YOU CAN SKI

Introduction

My purpose in writing this book is to help more people get more pleasure out of skiing. It was written for the beginner, intermediate and expert skier, but I hope it will also have some value for the professional ski instructor.

I do not intend to introduce you to a revolutionary new method of skiing but rather to a blended combination of well-known methods to which I have added a vital key action—the controlled knee. It makes every turn a simple maneuver. I am convinced, and hope to convince you, that skiing is similar to, and as easy as, walking.

For me learning to ski has not been easy. I've been at it thirty-five years, and I'm still learning, but in that time I think I have discovered the key to natural, controlled and secure skiing.

One of the chief causes of ski accidents is the fear which comes from insecurity. This insecurity stems from lack of knowledge. By giving you a clear understanding of how to turn your skis accurately, I hope to reduce your fears to a minimum and make you a secure and happy skier.

Those of you who have skied before, let me ask this: Can you stop on a dime? Would you like to be able to always make smooth turns and be in complete control throughout the turn? Is your speed always under control? Would you like to be able to keep your skis close together at all times? Do you wedeln with ease? Are you confused about what to do with your upper body while making a turn? Do you know your bad habits and how to get rid of them? Do you ski comfortably in deep snow or on ice? I hope to help you solve these problems naturally and easily.

Believe it or not, you can begin to learn to ski at home. Slowly walk the length of a room and turn. Think carefully about what you are doing. Be conscious of each movement. Notice the ease with which you shift your weight from one foot to the other. Now, and most important, notice how your upper body (shoulders and hips) "twists" slightly so that you "face" the about-to-be-weighted foot. Whether you have skied before or not, a clear understanding of this natural, involuntary "twisting" "facing" movement will help you immensely when you get on skis.

My method is based on five key actions: *Posture, Facing, Stepping, Kneeling* and *Twisting.* It is important that you learn the words, in the order given, and the actions they denote. The actions are thoroughly explained, in sequence, in the text.

In skiing, motivation and encouragement are everything. You must want to learn to ski or you never will. Your first couple of tries can be to please somebody else—husband, wife, children, etc.—but eventually you must do it to please yourself. Skiing is in the best sense a completely selfish sport. You will get encouragement from your friends and your ski instructor. If you have no friends (unlikely) or no ski instructor (foolish), encourage yourself.

I do not suggest that you learn to ski from this book alone. It is meant as an aid. You should take classes or individual instruction, preferably from a Certified Professional Ski Teacher. When you are in ski class, listen carefully to the explanation, feel out and try to remember the position the instructor places you in, then imitate him as well as you can.

To learn quickly, you must want to. Think positively; it is the key to success. You can absorb and retain skiing knowledge best by:

1. Listening and watching carefully.
2. Being placed in the correct positions.
3. Imitating repeatedly.

Class lessons, though less expensive, are naturally not quite as effective as individual lessons. Individual lessons help you especially if you are extremely self-conscious, have bad balance or if you have developed some bad habits. In group classes you have the advantage of skiing with others on your own level and learning from their mistakes.

Your hardest day on skis will be your first. Be patient with yourself. You may think you know what to do, but you will find that your body will not respond as you would like it to. It will take a while for your muscles to toughen up. There are some exercises in the text that will help you.

Beg, borrow or rent (skiers don't steal) equipment; if possible go to an area where there is a ski school staffed with professional ski instructors. Having read this book you will find, especially if you have tried the walking experiment, you are two jumps ahead of everyone else. Take lessons. Read the book at night by the fire; it may cause some arguments, but then the arguments will be about skiing, so that's all right. Now that you're a skier, you won't want to talk about anything else anyway. Best wishes for happy (and safe) skiing.

Part One

BEGINNER TO NOVICE

CHAPTER I

Ski Equipment

Ski first, buy later. Before you buy a lot of expensive equipment find out if you like to ski. Rent skis, boots and poles from a near-by ski shop, and take a few lessons, preferably from a certified ski instructor. By the second or third day you'll know whether or not to buy.

BOOTS

Ski boots are the most important and often the most expensive part of your equipment. You don't have to buy the best, but you must find a boot that meets the following important requirements:

1. It should be made of thick stiff leather for maximum ankle support.
2. The sole should be inflexible and should withstand any effort to bend or twist it.
3. The lacings should start from the base of the big toe.
4. The top of the boot should be two or three inches above the ankle joint.
5. After the boots have been laced you should be able to kneel easily without restriction, and your heel should stay in place, remaining flat on the floor of the boot. If necessary, the lacings at the top of the boot may be loosened. Also, when you tip your boot from side to side your heel should not wobble.
6. The boot should fit snugly around and under your ankle joint.
7. You should have enough room in the front of the boot to

wiggle your toes. If your toes are cramped against the walls of your boots your feet will get cold from lack of circulation.

8. Skiing in new boots can be painful. Here's what you can do about it: Before taking a bath put on the two pairs of socks you would ordinarily wear while skiing. Put on your boots, lace them up and get into the tub. Stay there for half an hour. Get out of the tub, dry yourself, put on a bathrobe and walk around the house in the wet boots for two hours. You may need someone to follow you around with a mop, but it will be worth it. The boots will mold themselves exactly to the shape of your feet. Take them off and put them on the boot clamps. Stuff them with newspaper; this will absorb the moisture. Put in fresh paper as needed. It will take several days for the boots to dry thoroughly, but if the above directions are carefully followed your boots will fit comfortably.

Most skiers put up with the pain of a new boot until it is gradually broken in to the form of their own foot. Be brave.

A word about socks: First put on a pair of ordinary gym socks; cover these with a heavy (heavier than the gym socks) pair of hand-knit, raw wool socks. Loosely woven material gives better insulation from the cold. Now put your boots on, lace them snugly and walk around. If you've given your boots the water treatment and your socks fit properly, the boots should feel comfortable.

Boot Maintenance

1. After skiing: dry the outside, and stuff the insides with newspaper to absorb the moisture.

2. Place the boots on boot clamps to keep the soles straight, and let them dry overnight *at room temperature only.*

3. Polish them each day before using. Use only ordinary shoe or boot polish containing wax. This will keep the moisture out and preserve the leather. *Do not use waterproofing or waterproofing agents on your boots.*

SKIS

American-made skis are excellent, and you have a choice of four different kinds: wooden, metal, plastic and fiber glass.

Wood

Look for straightness, strength, flexibility, a durable bottom and good edges.

1. To see if the skis are straight, place each ski on a flat level floor, running surface down. Gently try to rock the ski sideways from edge to edge. If it rocks it is warped. Don't use it; but especially don't buy it: it will hinder your turns. (Figs. 1 and 2)

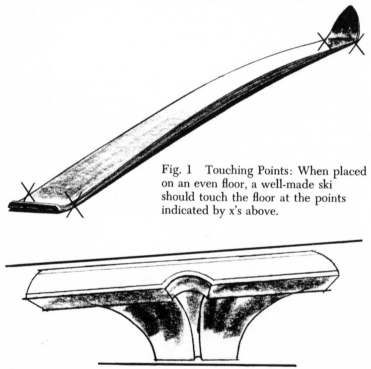

Fig. 1   Touching Points: When placed on an even floor, a well-made ski should touch the floor at the points indicated by x's above.

Fig. 2   Cross section of a warped ski.

2. For strength pick a laminated ski.

3. A ski is less tiring to ski on, and is easier to turn, if it is reasonably flexible. To test a ski's flexibility hold your right hand at the middle of the ski on its running surface; hold the ski tip firmly in your left hand, keeping the heel next to your right foot. With your right hand push down the ski smartly into a bend at mid-point and release. If it bends easily it is flexible; if it doesn't it is stiff. An even better way is to place one-and-a-half-inch blocks under the touching points of the skis and stand on the middle of them. If the ski is flexible it will touch the floor.

4. For a good durable bottom the running surface of the ski should be covered with plastic or Permacite. This will hold wax well and provide speed.

5. Your skis must have good steel edges. These are needed for gripping the ice, biting the snow and for climbing and turning.

Metal

If you can afford metal skis, by all means get a pair. They require relatively no maintenance (no blocking and clamping to hold their shape, as with wooden skis). The steel edges are put into the bottoms in one long section so that they cannot easily be ripped out by hitting a rock. Metal skis are strong, flexible and have a fast-sliding and durable running surface. They are more maneuverable than wooden skis and, for all day skiing, less tiring.

Plastic and Fiber glass

These skis are still in the experimental stage. When the manufacturers of plastic and fiber glass skis have ironed out the various problems they have had in using this material we may find them superior to wooden or metal skis.

A short note on short skis for beginners and very short skis in general:

A beginning skier should use a shorter pair of skis than is ordinarily used. To avoid the necessity of buying two pairs, the beginner should rent skis for his first few lessons. The way to decide on the size of the ski is this: When you stretch the arm straight up over the head, the top of the ski should reach somewhere between the elbow and the wrist. Remember, this method of measuring is for beginners only. Many people may choose a shorter ski; but I'd advise that it be not shorter than your height.

Very short skis (two and a half feet) are on the market. While they may make learning to ski easier and they are relatively easy to turn, short skis are unstable and are not recommended for high speeds; they do not give the skier a steady smooth ride nor do they grip ice as well as the long ski. In addition, the person who learns on a very short ski will eventually have to adjust to a somewhat longer ski and still again to a regulation-size ski. However, they are a novel plaything and fun to have as an extra part of your ski equipment.

BINDINGS

Ski bindings hold your boot to the ski. You should wear release bindings. A good binding is simple to adjust, has few moving parts and will keep its adjustment while you are skiing. Test your bindings and make sure they release when tested. Bindings should be hand-tested at the beginning of each ski day. Do not use a safety clip. It is cheaper but apt to break or, worse, cause the ski to pinwheel, possibly injuring you. Use an Arlberg strap, which is made of leather and fastens on to the cables of your bindings and wraps around your foot to give more ankle support. When your safety bindings open after a fall, the Arlberg strap prevents the ski from "running away." A runaway ski is a hazard to other skiers.

Mounting Bindings

1. First, place the ski horizontally on the back edge of a kitchen knife so that neither tip touches the floor. Mark the top. This is your balance point.

2. Find the two touch points of the unweighted ski by laying the ski flat on a level floor.

3. Measure the distance between both touch in half. Mark the top. This is your touch point.

4. Measure the halfway mark between the bala. the touch point. Mark the top of the ski. This is the piv your ski.

5. Measure the length of the bottom of your boot. Div half and make a mark on the side of the sole. This is the ᴨ   ᴅ-point of your boot.

6. Place the mid-point of your boot two and a half inches to the rear of the ski from the pivot point. The ball, or pivot point, of your foot should now be directly over the pivot point of your ski.

7. Mount your bindings in conformity with the boot's correct position on your ski. Mounting your bindings at this position will give you maximum control.

POLES

Ski poles are vitally necessary for good skiing. They help your lateral balance, assist you while climbing and give you an additional lift and balance while executing high speed turns. The length of the poles is an individual matter. Most good skiers prefer the top of the pole to reach the mid-point between their armpit and 'the top of their shoulder; others like them shorter, as much as two inches below this point. Poles which are too short, though easier to handle, will cause you to bend from the waist instead of from the knee, a very bad habit to get into.

WAX

Wax is bought in solid form, but it is applied either as a liquid or as a solid. The liquid does a more lasting job, but it is time-consuming to apply. You must first melt the wax down into a liquid and then coat the skis with a small brush applicator and wait until they dry. The solid wax comes in a bar which you simply crayon on. You should use it indoors. The warmth softens ne wax and makes it easier to apply. Start from the heel of your ski and wax the running surface moving toward the tip. Rub wax in the groove as well. Proper waxing minimizes sticking to the snow and allows the ski to run smoothly. When metal skis are waxed, they tend to go too fast for a beginner to control. Nonlaminated wooden skis should be waxed almost every time you go skiing. Most skiers use laminated skis, and these skis will usually require wax only in sudden changes of temperature or when it is raining or snowing. Follow the simple rule listed below:

HARD WAX—when the temperature suddenly drops; for dry, nonsnowballing snow.

MEDIUM WAX—when it is near freezing; for changing snow conditions.

SOFT WAX—when there is a thaw; for sticky, clogging snow.

You should always have with you on the slopes a piece of graphite or silver paraffin wax for use when your skis are not gliding smoothly.

SKI CLOTHES

Ski pants, sweaters, parkas and ski mittens should be warm, windproof and water repellent. Winter underwear is strongly recommended. Remember when buying ski clothes, you want them to last and withstand rough wear and to keep you warm and comfortable all day. The same, of course, for children. Make sure that the quality of the material and workmanship will withstand heavy wear by getting authentic ski clothes, those manufactured specifically for skiing.

HOW TO CARRY YOUR SKIS

First, place the running surfaces together; put the skis on your left shoulder, ski tips in front. Keep the bindings slightly behind your ear. Keep the skis on their sides, and grab them with your left hand, near the tips. If the skis seem too heavy and uncom-

Fig. 3   Use your poles to take some of the weight of the skis off your shoulder.

fortable, do this: Place the two poles together in your right hand, tuck the basket ends of the poles under the heels of the skis while putting the shafts on your right shoulder. By applying a slight downward leverage on the handles of the poles you will be able

Fig. 4   Indoors, carry your skis vertically.

to lift the skis slightly, taking some of the weight from your left shoulder. (Fig. 3)

When going in and out of buildings carry your skis vertically. (Fig. 4) Otherwise, they can be a dangerous weapon.

CHAPTER II

If You Can Walk
You Can Ski!

Skiing can be as simple as walking. Putting one foot in front of another is as natural as breathing, but have you ever stopped to consider what is involved in this basic act? Do you understand how you walk up or down a hill or how you turn a corner? An understanding of the mechanics of walking will help you immeasurably when you begin to ski.

There are four basic actions involved in walking in a straight line, five when we consider walking turns. These movements are the five key steps in learning how to ski:

1. *Posture:* Body erect, knees slightly bent.
2. *Facing:* Facing the foot you are stepping onto.
3. *Stepping:* Shifting your weight *from* the ball of the foot you are stepping off *to* the ball of the foot you are stepping onto.
4. *Kneeling:* Bending and turning in the knee of the leg you are stepping onto.
5. *Twisting:* Pivoting the foot you are stepping onto while counterrotating your upper body (rotating it in the opposite direction).

Try the following simple experiment in your own home; it is your first lesson in skiing.

HOW WE WALK

1. Stand erect, weight evenly distributed.

2. Unlock your knees and bend them forward slightly. This will bring your weight (two separate masses: chest and hips) over the balls of your feet. (*Posture*–Fig. 5)

3. In order to move the left foot forward you must put all your weight on the right foot so the unweighted left foot can be lifted and moved ahead. As you move the left foot forward your whole upper body will turn slightly in the direction you are stepping. (*Facing*)

4. Put your unweighted left foot down, keeping the entire weight of your body on the ball of your right foot. (Fig. 6) Now, move your right knee forward slightly and transfer your weight to the ball of your left foot. (*Stepping*) As you do this bend your left knee slightly to receive or catch the weight. (*Kneeling*–Fig. 7) It's the same principle as catching a ball with a glove: the glove, controlled by your hand, *gives* a little to cushion the shock of the thrown ball.

That was walking in a straight line. Now let's add a turn. Go through the same movements, but as you are *Stepping* and *Kneeling*, pivot your left foot clockwise. (*Twisting*) You have made a right "parallel" turn the same way you would on skis.

You are now ready to ski.

GETTING READY TO SKI

If you take your skis outdoors from a warm building do not immediately set them in the snow. Wait ten minutes. If you put warm skis down in the snow, ice will form on the bottoms and they will not slide.

Now that you have given the skis, and yourself, a chance to

Fig. 5 LEFT. *Posture:* Body erect, knees slightly bent. Fig. 6 CENTER. Ready to *Step:* Weight on the ball of the right foot, left foot unweighted. Fig. 7 RIGHT. *Stepping* and *Kneeling:* Left knee slightly bent to catch the shifted weight.

adjust to the cold lay them down in the snow, preferably on a flat level area. Putting on skis for the first time is a new experience—you will need a friend. If you are alone, remember that skiers are friendly people, always willing to help a beginner. If you're shy, someone from the ski shop will help you. The most important thing is to make sure your release bindings are properly adjusted. To test the release of your bindings you should do the following:

Fig. 8   Ski boot with a properly fastened Alberg strap.

1. After your boots have been fastened to the bindings wrap the Arlberg Strap around your boots and fasten the clasp. (Fig. 8)

2. Then strike *sharply* with the heel of your hand against the inside of your boot, near the front. (Fig. 9)

3. The front safety release should open, and your boot should twist free. (Fig. 10)

4. If the binding does not release, loosen the adjustment on the swivel at the toe of the boot. If the binding releases too easily, tighten the adjustment.

Now that you have your skis on, pick up your poles. (The first day you may have to have someone hand them to you.) Slide your hand up the shaft toward the leather handgrip. Put your hand through the handgrip loop so your fingers are facing upward and the strap is around your wrist. (Fig. 11) Now grab the loop and the handle of the pole at the same time. (Fig. 12) This is the correct way to hold your poles.

Fig. 9   Sharply strike the side of your boot with the heel of your hand.

Fig. 10   If your safety binding is properly adjusted, your boot twists free.

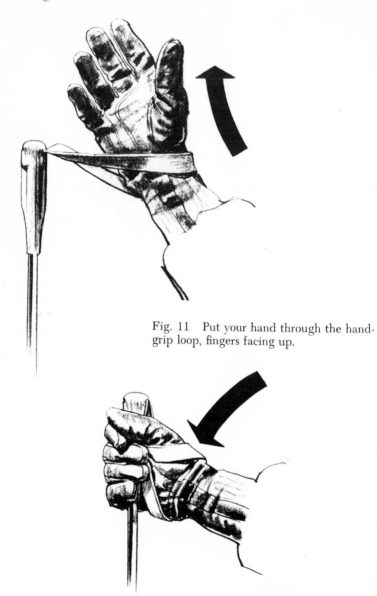

Fig. 11   Put your hand through the handgrip loop, fingers facing up.

Fig. 12   Grab the loop and the handle at the same time.

HOW TO WALK WITH SKIS ON

LESSON 3

1. Stand erect with your weight evenly distributed.

2. Unlock your knees, supporting yourself with your poles. (*Posture*) Push your left foot forward slightly (do not lift) so that it glides along the surface of the snow. (Fig. 13) As you do this your body will naturally face in the direction of the left ski. (*Facing*–Fig. 14)

3. Bring the ski to a stop. Turned slightly in the direction of the left ski, press down on the ball of the left foot as you push your weight forward (as in the walking exercise) from the ball of your right foot. (*Stepping*)

4. Bending your right knee and your right ankle will help you shift your weight to the left foot. The left knee should be slightly bent to receive the newly shifted weight. (*Kneeling*–Fig. 15)

5. Now push the unweighted right foot along the snow in a gliding motion. (*Facing*–Fig. 16)

Bending your knees is an important protection against skiing accidents. Knees properly bent are like shock-absorbing car springs: they will absorb the shock of bumps, hollows and uneven terrain. Do your feet and ankles feel weak? Do not be alarmed, this is a very natural reaction. Walk around a bit on level ground with your skis on; this will strengthen your foot muscles and improve your balance. Do your skis seem heavy and long, clumsy and hostile? Be patient. In a very short time they will seem a natural, and friendly, extension of your own body. Remember: your first few days of skiing are the most difficult; it is natural to feel clumsy and awkward and that your muscles are weak (they probably are); and again: be patient.

Fig. 13   Push your left foot forward slightly; do not lift it—let it glide.

Fig. 14 *Facing* the left ski.

Fig. 15 *Stepping* and *Kneeling*, bending the left knee to receive the newly shifted weight.

Fig. 16   Push the unweighted right ski along the snow.

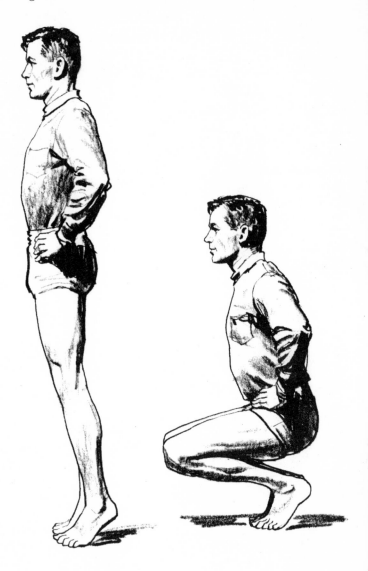

Fig. 17   LEFT. Raise your heels until you are standing on tiptoe.

Fig. 18   RIGHT. Squatting position.

Exercises

To ski comfortably and safely your foot and leg muscles must be in reasonably strong condition. Any exercise you do to help strengthen these muscles will help; here are two of the best:

Stand erect, weight evenly distributed. Keeping your body and knees straight, slowly raise your heels until you are standing tiptoe. (Fig. 17) Now, keeping your body and knees straight, lower your heels slowly until they touch the floor. Increase the number of lifts each day until you can do fifty in succession.

To strengthen your knees and legs: stand erect with your feet about three inches apart, feet turned out. Keeping your upper body straight, slowly bend your knees while lifting your heels until you are in a squatting position. (Fig. 18) Do not bend at the waist. Keeping your body straight, slowly raise yourself to a standing position. Daily increase the number of times until you reach twenty-five.

HOW TO TURN ON LEVEL GROUND

LESSON 4

1. Remembering good *Posture* (body erect, knees slightly bent), lift up the tip of your right ski by lifting your toes in the boot; keep the heel or rear of the ski on the snow. Move the ski out (away from you) a short distance to the right. (Fig. 19) Set the ski down on the snow and place your weight on it. (*Stepping*)

2. *Facing* your left foot, pick up the tip of your left ski, leaving the heel in the snow, and bring it around parallel to the right ski. (*Stepping*–Fig. 20)

3. A series of these steps in the same direction will bring you around full circle. (Fig. 21) Practice this a number of times in both directions until you can do it easily.

Fig. 19   LEFT. Lift the tip of your right ski and move it a short distance to your right.

Fig. 20   RIGHT. Bring the left ski around parallel to your right ski.

Practice walking on level ground, and combine this with the turn described above. Your upper body should act on skis the same way it does in ordinary walking: arms loose at your sides moving opposite to your feet to equalize the distribution of your weight. As your left foot goes forward, your right arm swings

Fig. 21   Lift the tip of your ski again and move it. (A series of these moves will turn you around.)

forward the same distance. Notice that this forces the body to face slightly in the direction of the foot which is to be set down. The ski pole point should be put in the snow slightly behind or even with, but not in front of, the opposite forward foot (right pole, left foot; left pole, right foot; etc.).

FALLING AND GETTING UP

LESSON 5

If you haven't fallen yet, you've got good balance. If you fell, were you able to get up without help? If you did, you're doing very well; it's not easy.

If you feel yourself falling, try to fall slightly back and to the side of your skis (either side). Keep your skis and your body as far away from each other as possible. Try to relax as you go down and don't panic. The stronger your muscles, the less often you will fall; but remember, even the best skiers fall. Practice falling and getting up several times. Does it seem silly? It isn't.

How to Get Up from a Fall

1. Your first impulse will be to scramble up any old way. Don't. You may find you have just set yourself up for another fall or, worse, you may find yourself going down the slope at a

Fig. 22   LEFT. Uphill hand on the baskets of the poles, downhill hand on the shafts.

Fig. 23   RIGHT. Push the uphill edges of your skis into the side of the slope.

speed you are unable to handle. Take a second to find out where you are in relation to the slope. Move your skis around so they are parallel to each other and, most important, lying directly across the slope.

2. Take your poles off your wrists and put the spike of one pole through the ring, or basket, of the other so that the two poles are now one.

3. Roll yourself into a ball by pulling your knees up to your chest.

4. Force your skis back under you as much as possible, but keep them parallel and across the slope.

5. Put the spikes of your poles into the snow beside the hip on the upper slope. The shafts of your poles should be across your lap.

6. Put your uphill hand on the baskets of the poles and your downhill hand high up on the shafts. (Fig. 22)

7. Push the uphill edges of your skis into the side of the slope. (Fig. 23)

Fig. 24   LEFT. Push your body diagonally forward.

Fig. 25   RIGHT. When you have pushed your body until it is directly over your feet, you should be able to stand erect.

8. Gripping the poles, push your entire body diagonally forward so your body is over your feet. (Fig. 24)

9. If you have pushed your body into the proper position— over your feet—you should be able to stand erect without falling. (Fig. 25)

If you fall several times in the course of trying to follow the above instructions don't be discouraged. You are probably trying to get up too fast. Be patient with yourself and do it slowly, a step at a time. There is usually some spot or position in the snow to place your poles where you will find the best leverage for pushing. If you take the time and effort to find it, getting up will be easier.

Practice

Practice walking, gliding and turning (stepping around) until the skis feel a bit more comfortable. Make sure the weighted ski is turned very slightly on its inside edge. If your ankle is turned out (putting your weight on the outside edge) you will fall. Try standing on one foot; then try coasting a bit, first on one foot and then on the other. Continue to think about your *Posture, Facing, Stepping* and *Kneeling.* Use your poles as you walk. Push on your right pole to shift your weight to your left foot. Let the skis glide. Push in with your left pole and push your right foot forward. By this time you should be having some fun.

SKATING ON SKIS

LESSON 6

To learn to balance yourself on one ski, you should practice the skating step, on nearly flat terrain. It is similar to ice skating.

From a standing position lift your right ski off the ground an inch or so. Turn the ski slightly to your right so that the rear of your right ski crosses, in the air, the rear or heel of your left ski. (Fig. 26) Move the right ski (the one in the air) far enough forward to avoid stepping on the rear of the left ski. (*Facing*) Now step diagonally forward onto the right ski, pushing yourself with your poles and from the inside edge of your left ski and straightening your left knee. You are actually pushing yourself away from your left ski in a forward *Stepping* position in order

Fig. 26   Lift your right ski off the ground two inches and turn it to the right so that it crosses the heel of your left ski in the air.

that you may put all your weight on your right ski. (*Kneeling*)
Your left ski will automatically tip slightly on its inside edge.
This edging will give you added pushing power. Straightening
your left knee from its proper bent position will move your
weight diagonally forward toward the right ski. (Fig. 27) Coast
on the right ski with the right knee slightly bent in the direction

Fig. 27   Straighten your left knee, and your weight will move diagonally forward toward your right ski.

the ski is headed. You should be balanced entirely on your right foot. The knee should be bent forward and in; the kneecap should be directly over the ball of the foot. As you coast, lift the left ski and bring it alongside the right one. (Fig. 28) Now lift and turn your left ski a little to the outside. Set the left ski down at an angle and far enough forward to prevent stepping on the

Fig. 28 As you coast along, lift your left ski and bring it up to your right one.

rear of the right ski. (*Facing*) Now push with your poles and from the inside edge of your right ski, while straightening the right knee; this should transfer your weight to the ball of the left foot. (*Stepping* and *Kneeling*) Remember the action words in order: *Posture, Facing, Stepping* and *Kneeling*. If you followed the directions carefully you have been skating on skis.

This pleasant and rewarding exercise is great for improving your balance. Also, it prepares you for parallel skiing by teaching you to ski on one foot.

THE RUNNING POSITION—POSTURE

LESSON 7

Finally you find yourself at the top of a slight grade or incline. You will experience a new and pleasant sensation. The skis slide on the snow by themselves, leaving the upper part of your body behind. Unless you are prepared for this surprise, you may lose your balance and fall. To keep your balance, your chest and hips (hereafter referred to as your weight) must be in alignment and perpendicular to your skis. Since balance is more difficult to achieve on an incline, your weight must be placed exactly over the center of the skis. In order to arrive in this position bend your knees slightly forward; the lower part of your leg will automatically bend forward at the ankle, and your weight will move forward as a unit. The hips and chest should now be lined up directly over the center, or pivot point, of the ski. The steeper the slope, the more your weight must be tilted forward to remain perpendicular to the pivot point of the skis.

This is the fundamental position for proper balance on an incline. It is commonly known as the running position. I call it *Posture*. This is your first action word. Soon this position will be second nature. (Fig. 29) To learn correct *Posture,* you must avoid some common mistakes. (Fig. 30)

Fig. 29 *Posture:* The correct Running position.

Fig. 30   Common mistakes in running position: *A.* Weight too far back on heels, pelvis tipped forward, causing a hollow back. *B.* Body not erect, bending at waist. *C.* Body not erect, knees bent too much.

CLIMBING ON SKIS

LESSON 8

To slide down a hill you must first climb up it. If you just aim your skis up the hill and start climbing you won't get very far: you'll slide backward with every step, which is dangerous. Here are two methods for climbing correctly:

Sidestep

1. Aim your skis across the hill at right angles to the fall line (steepest line of slope). Bite into the snow with the uphill edge of each ski.

2. Lift the uphill ski (heel and tip) and move it sideways uphill a short distance. (Fig. 31) Set it down hard, using the uphill edge to get a grip on the snow. Your weight should then be on the uphill ski.

3. Bring the downhill ski up and parallel with the uphill ski, again using the uphill edge (of the downhill ski) to get a grip on the snow. (Fig. 32) Continue in this way until you reach the top of the hill.

Fig. 31   FACING PAGE. Lift the uphill ski (heel *and* toe) and move it sideways up the hill a short distance.

Fig. 32   Lift the downhill ski and bring it up and parallel with the uphill ski.

Sidestep Traverse

The sidestep traverse allows you to go up and across the hill at the same time.

1. At the base of the hill put your skis together, and parallel; aim them to the left of the slope.

2. *Face* and lift your right (uphill) ski slightly off the snow. To pick up your ski evenly you will have to lift your toes in the boot. Move the ski forward *and* up the hill one step; keep it parallel with the left (downhill) ski. As you set it down in the snow aim your bending knee slightly uphill; this will tip your ski on its outside edge. (Fig. 33)

3. Press the uphill, outside edge of your right ski into the snow to get a grip, or bite. Place all your weight on it. (*Stepping*)

Fig. 33 Ready to *Step:* Right ski forward and up a step, knee bent outward slightly.

4. With all your weight on the right uphill ski lift your left (downhill) ski, bring it forward a step, and it should be parallel with the other ski. Tilt the left knee forward and in at a slight angle. (Fig. 34) The uphill edge of the left ski will then bite into the snow. Put your weight on the left ski and repeat the process. You will, of course, use your poles to help you walk.

The sidestep traverse is reasonably comfortable and less tiring than other methods of climbing. This method will take you up the hill at an angle. As a beginner, how high up the hill should you go? Look back frequently; the nervous feeling in the pit of your stomach will tell you when to stop. Before climbing any higher feel certain that you will be able to ski down from where you are without falling.

Fig. 34   Bring your unweighted left ski up parallel to the uphill ski and bend your left knee slightly inward.

STARTING POSITION

LESSON 9

Let's suppose you are on the hill at right angles to the line of the slope. To get into a position to ski downhill can be difficult. Here's how:

1. Put both poles into the snow, downhill, about two feet apart. (Fig. 35)

2. Leaving the pole spikes in position, swing the pole shafts, with your hands closed over butt ends of poles, toward your waist so that you can put all your weight on them. Using the poles, push and step back uphill. (Fig. 36) Step your skis around slowly until they are aimed directly downhill and are parallel to each other. The tips of your skis should be between the two dug-in poles. Your poles are keeping you from coasting down the hill, so keep your elbows locked.

Fig. 35 FACING PAGE. Put both poles in the snow, downhill, about two feet apart.

Fig. 36 Using your poles to hold you back, aim directly downhill, skis slightly apart. (Note hands on top of poles.)

3. You are now ready to put your body in the correct running position. Keeping your right arm locked, lift the left pole and set it in the snow halfway between the tip of the ski and the boot. Quickly bring the right pole back and set it even with the left one. As you do this, you will find your body straightening. (Fig. 37)

Fig. 37   Correct Starting Position: Knees bent, body erect, poles in snow.

4. As you straighten your back, bend your knees.

5. Lift up the poles and hold them off the ground behind you. (Fig. 38) You're off.

Fig. 38 Correct Running Position: Knees bent, body erect, pelvis tipped back, poles lifted by tightening little finger.

CLIMBING ON SKIS (II)

LESSON 10

Herringbone

The herringbone is another method of climbing. It leaves a pattern on the snow like a herringbone.

Fig. 39   Facing uphill with your skis in a "V" and your poles behind you, lift your left ski, aiming it at an angle away from your body.

1. Face the hill and separate the fronts of your skis. They will form a V.

2. Turn your ankles in. This will set your skis on their inside edges.

3. Place your poles behind you, and put your hands on top of the handles. Holding your poles this way will give you the supporting leverage you need.

4. Lift your left ski; keep it aimed away from your body at an angle. (Fig. 39) Set it down one step forward in the snow on its

Fig. 40 With your weight on the inside edge of your left ski, lift your right ski and aim it at an angle away from your body.

inside edge. Really bite the snow with the ski. It will make a mark on the snow like a tiny stair step.

5. Put all your weight on the left ski.

6. Pick up your right ski, advance and aim it to the right. (Fig. 40) Set it down hard and move your weight in that direction.

The herringbone climb is done with a slight rocking motion as your weight shifts from one ski to the other. It should be used for short climbs on gentle slopes. It can be tiring if done for too long.

Fig. 41   Starting position for a kick turn: Skis parallel, poles at tips and heels of skis.

KICK TURN

<small>LESSON</small> 11

You are now ready to learn the kick turn. Try it on level ground in both directions. After you have mastered it try it on a gentle rise. When doing it on a hill *Face* and kick the downhill ski, not the uphill one.

1. Stand erect with your skis parallel and together.

2. *Face* your right ski; poles in hand, stretch your arms out horizontally.

3. Put the spike of your left pole next to the outside tip of the left ski. Put the spike of your right pole next to the outside heel of the right ski. (Fig. 41)

Fig. 42   Scuff your right ski back and forth.

Fig. 43   Kick your right ski forward and plant the heel in the snow, weight completely on left foot, supported by poles.

Fig. 44 Turn the right ski completely around.

4. Scuff your right ski backward and forward a bit. (Fig. 42)
Then kick the ski up and out in front of you with some force so
that the heel of the right ski is in the snow even with the tip of
the left ski. You are supporting yourself with the two poles, and
your weight should be entirely on your left foot. (Fig. 43) Immediately turn your right foot to the right, putting your right ski
on the snow. Figs. 44 and 45) This is an awkward position, but
you will be out of it in a minute. The tip of the right ski is now
facing directly behind you.

Fig. 45   Lay the right ski on the ground parallel to the left ski, but facing in the opposite direction.

Fig. 46   FACING PAGE TOP. Having brought the left pole around to the right and put your weight on the right leg, swing the left ski around to the right.

Fig. 47   BOTTOM. Put the left ski down parallel to the right one.

5. Bring your left pole around to your right, stick it in the snow about two feet to the left of the tip of your right ski. Press down on both poles and shift your weight to your right foot.

6. Gently pick up your left ski by raising your toes. Keeping the knee straight, swing the left ski around to the right. (Fig. 46) Set it down parallel to the right ski in the new direction. (Fig. 47)

You have made a 180-degree turn. Congratulations!

CHAPTER III

How to Slow Down

If you have followed the instructions in the preceding lessons and practiced thoroughly the various maneuvers you should be feeling more comfortable on skis and ready for the Snowplow and Snowplow Stop.

SNOWPLOW

LESSON 1

Pick a very gentle slope with a flat runout, a beginners' slope, in fact. Climb it using one of the methods learned in the last chapter. When you reach the top, step your skis around and aim them downhill. Using your poles to keep you from taking off, get into the Starting Position: upper body straight and perpendicular to the center of the skis, knees slightly bent. Lift your poles, swing them behind you. (*Posture*) Lift your hands and carry them slightly ahead of you. Keep your weight evenly distributed. You are now skiing downhill in the Running Position (schussing). Do not look at your skis; look about twenty feet ahead. Try to relax, but above all *enjoy the ride*.

Try this several times, and remember: bend your knees, keep your upper body erect, do not bend at the waist, do not look at your ski tips; look straight ahead.

1. This time, as you go down slowly, try to push the rear ends of your skis apart. As you do this, lower your whole body, while still keeping it erect, by bending your knees more.

2. At the same time, using the muscles in the front part of your feet, keep the tips of your skis close together, but do not allow them to cross. As you go, edge the skis in slightly. (Fig. 48)

Note: When you begin pushing the rear of the skis apart the skis must be nearly flat on the snow, ever so slightly edged inward. As the rear of your skis gets further and further apart and your knees bend further forward your skis will begin to edge in. This edging is what slows you down. Be sure not to push the outside edges into the snow. They will catch and you might fall.

Because of the special kind of thrill that comes from being able to control your own downhill speed you will not have to be told to practice the above exercise until you do it perfectly; you will actually enjoy practicing. You are on your way to controlling your skis—to becoming a skier.

Fig. 48 Snowplow position: Knees bent, body erect, skis in an inverted "V" and edged in slightly.

SNOWPLOW STOP

LESSON 2

1. Start down the hill in a Snowplow position.
2. Shift your weight from its position over the balls of your feet to a point directly over the heels.
3. As you move your weight back, bend your knees while spreading the heels of the skis wide apart. This will cause the skis to edge gradually so that they will slow up and then stop. The faster you do this, the faster you will stop. (Fig. 49)

Note: This is one of the few times in skiing when you move your weight back instead of forward.

Practice the Snowplow until you can go as fast and as slow as you please; practice it in combination with schussing (not too fast yet) and the Snowplow Stop, and practice the Snowplow Stop until you can stop exactly where you wish.

Fig. 49   Snowplow Stop: Moving your weight back, push your heels out, while edging your skis until you stop.

Part Two

NOVICE TO INTERMEDIATE

CHAPTER IV

Turns

TURNING WHILE WALKING

LESSON 1

By now the muscles of your knees, ankles and feet are stronger, your coordination and sense of balance have improved and your responses are quicker. (If you have been following the course of instruction with any degree of concentration, this is true even though you may not be aware of the improvement.) Before you attempt a turn on skis, it will be of enormous help to you to examine how you make a turn when you are not on skis. Since a marching turn, like a ski turn, should be executed with the utmost economy of motion, we will use a right flank turn as an example.

The right flank movement begins when (1) the right foot strikes the ground, continues through (2) one more stride forward, when (3) the left or leading foot pivots clockwise, and is completed with (4) the right or trailing foot stepping to the right.

Let's examine this pivot turn more carefully. The movements you will be making are similar to those you will make in parallel skiing and turning. The following experiment can be done in the ski lodge or in the privacy of your living room. Let's do the right flank turn, step by step:

1. Step forward onto your right foot. (*Posture*)
2. Slowly move your left foot forward and set it down heel first. (Fig. 50) As you bring your weight diagonally forward onto the left foot your body will involuntarily face it slightly. (*Facing*)
3. Gradually apply weight to the ball of the left foot by moving the entire body forward from the ball of the right foot. (*Stepping*)
4. Bend the left knee slightly to receive the weight of the body. (*Kneeling*–Fig. 51)
5. As you bend the left knee pivot on the left foot, twisting it clockwise. (*Twisting*–Fig. 52)
6. Advance the unweighted right foot and put it down in the new direction. (Fig. 53)

You have just made a right-hand turn. This little experiment may seem silly and unimportant; it is not. If you try the above action several times, both to the right and to the left, and examine carefully the dynamics of each separate movement you will be well on your way to parallel skiing.

Why learn to turn on skis at all? If you stand on the top of a steep slope and look straight down the feeling in the pit of your stomach will tell you why. You must learn to turn in order to control your speed. If, standing at the top of the same slope, you do not get the feeling in the pit of your stomach but instead put your skis together and go, you will find yourself shooting downhill at an ever-increasing speed, unable to control your speed or your balance, a menace to other skiers, a danger to yourself and a potential hospital case. Even the best skiers do not ski straight down a slope. They are constantly turning even though their turns may be so small as to be almost invisible. So, you must learn to turn in order to constantly change your direction and get yourself safely down the hill. One further illustration: If you were walking down the same slope in summer you would not walk straight down; if you did you would end up going so fast

Fig. 50   LEFT. *Facing:* Move your left foot forward and set it down heel first.

Fig 51   RIGHT. *Stepping* and *Kneeling:* Put your weight on the ball of the left foot, bending your left knee, slightly.

Fig. 52   LEFT. *Twisting:* As you bend your left knee, pivot with your left foot.

Fig. 53   RIGHT. Advance the unweighted right foot and put it down in the new direction.

you would fall. Hiking down a mountain in summer you constantly switch back and forth gripping the ground with the inside edge of your downhill foot. The same is true in skiing: if you constantly change the direction of your skis and move across rather than down the slope you will reduce your speed. It is incorrect to think that edging the skis alone is the way to stop or slow down. Gradually edging the ski by bending the knee forward and in at an angle, plus sideslipping, skidding, drifting and scraping during the turn, is what makes you slow down.

Before you begin downhill skiing, it is important for you to know the dynamics of the pivot turn you make in ordinary walking, and to have an awareness of the laws of gravity which are constantly pulling your body downhill and some knowledge of your natural tendencies toward self-preservation.

In walking, your weight moves forward as you step ahead. You must also do this while skiing in order to reach the balance

Fig. 54   Do NOT bend
from the waist.

point and to make you more secure while gravity pulls you, at an ever-increasing speed, down the slope. If edged, even slightly, the wide or front part of the ski, called the "shovel," will cut or carve out your turn, if your weight is well forward. You must also turn the ski by *Kneeling* and *Twisting* as you bring your weight forward.

There are three natural tendencies that you must be aware of and must be prepared to counteract.

When you make your first straight run down a hill, as your speed increases you will have a tendency to bend from the waist. This is natural: you will want to get closer to the ground so you won't have so far to fall. *Do not bend from the waist.* (Fig. 54) Stand erect and bend your knees and ankles (Posture) to provide your body with that shock-absorbing spring we talked of earlier. (Fig. 55)

Fig. 55 Stand erect, with knees and ankles bent for shock-absorbing spring.

When you turn on level ground, you step on the whole foot, weight evenly distributed; when you turn on skis, gradually put all your weight on the ball of the foot, just behind the big toe. This puts the ski on a slight inside edge so that you can put all your weight on the ski without having it slide out from under you. (Fig. 56) *Do not flatten the ski as you are in the process of Stepping on it.* (Fig. 57)

Fig. 56   Edge the ski slightly so that it won't slide out from under you when you put your weight on it.

Fig. 57 Do NOT flatten your skis while *Stepping*.

Your third problem will be your tendency to bank your body inside as you go around a corner. This is the way you steer a bicycle and the way you water ski. While skiing down a hill, however, you must tip your body outside or downhill as you turn a corner. Your body must be perpendicular to the slope in order to get a more secure grip on the snow. *Do not lean in.* (Fig. 58) Lean out. (Fig. 59)

Fig. 58   Do NOT lean inside on a turn.

Fig. 59   DO lean out on a turn.

TURNING ON SKIS

LESSON 2

You have learned to slow down by using the Snowplow and you have learned to stop by using the Snowplow Stop. In both cases your weight was evenly distributed. You must now learn to put all your weight on one ski as you would put all your weight on one foot while walking down a hill.

Remember the five key steps you learned at the beginning of Chapter 2: *Posture, Facing, Stepping, Kneeling, Twisting.* The blending of these five actions will enable you to turn with precision and control.

The Snowplow Turn

1. From a good *Posture* position (knees slightly bent, body erect) begin slowly going down the hill in a Snowplow. Your speed is being controlled by your inside edges. (Fig. 60)

Note: Your good *Posture* position prevents you from bending at the waist.

2. You are going to turn left by shifting your weight to the right ski; but before you do, turn your shoulders and hips (your entire upper body) in the direction of the right ski. This is the second or *Facing* action. (Fig. 61)

Note: This will counteract your natural tendency to bank into the hill. You will be cooperating with the centrifugal force by *Facing* out (away from the hill).

3. Stay in the *Facing* position and gradually shift all of your weight to the ball of the right foot behind the big toe by bending the right knee. This changing of the weight completely from one ski to the other is known as the *Stepping* action. In shifting your weight, your natural tendency is to step on the whole foot at once. Do not flatten the foot; gradually apply your weight to the ball of the foot only. The *left* ski's inside edge, however, should tend to flatten.

Fig. 60 Snowplow position ready to turn: Knees bent, body erect, skis in an inverted "V" and edged in slightly. (Note weight slightly on left foot.)

Fig. 61   *Facing:* To turn to the left, face the right ski.

Fig. 62   FACING PAGE. *Stepping* and *Kneeling:* Shift your weight onto the ball of the right foot, behind the big toe, while bending your right knee in the direction of the turn.

4. As the weight is being shifted to the right ski, the bent right knee acts as a shock absorber and thus receives the weight without jarring the body. This is the *Kneeling* position. (Fig. 62)

Look what has happened! You've turned.

Fig. 63   *Twisting:* As you are *Stepping* and *Kneeling*, pivot the right foot slightly for greater control.

5. While you are in the process of *Kneeling* and *Stepping*— shifting your weight gradually forward onto the right (downhill) ski—*Twist* (pivot) the right foot counterclockwise slightly. (Fig. 63) This *Twisting* movement, the last of the five actions, is not

essential for the Snowplow Turn; proper shift of weight alone will turn you. It does, however, allow you greater control of the turn's direction and degree, and using it here will give you some necessary practice in blending the five basic actions in parallel skiing.

Summary: To turn in a Snowplow position begin with good *Posture; Face* the ski you are going to shift your weight to; *Step* on the ski, holding its edge while allowing the other ski to flatten; bend the *Knee* to catch the oncoming weight; *Twist* the foot in the desired direction.

In the beginning you may have difficulty in *Facing and Stepping* onto the right-hand ski. In moving your body away from the left, or uphill, ski you may be inadvertently stiffening the left leg; this will cause the left ski to edge on its right side, not allowing it to turn easily, if at all. To correct this, bend the left knee and force it to stay bent and aimed in the direction you are headed (left). Bending your left knee to the left (for a left turn) not only will flatten the ski, but also will help keep it even with the right ski while the two are being turned together. Notice that during the turn the right knee is bent and aimed slightly to the left, toward the tip of the left ski. This off-center knee-bend action, which is even more important in parallel turns, is called a controlled knee bend. It is the key to security in your turns.

If you examine the *Kneeling* action closely and in detail you will see what effect it has on your turns. By *Kneeling* forward yet inward at an angle as you step on one ski, your kneecap will move directly over the ball of the foot behind the big toe. Let's take a left turn. The angle of the right kneebend slightly tips the right ski on to the left portion of its running surface. The more you bend your knee at an angle, the more the ski edges and the more secure your grip on the incline is. Bending the knee at an angle off-center to the ski forces the foot to twist, with the result that the ski turns in the direction toward which the knee bends. If, however, you edge your ski too much, it will make a rut and set its own course—a long sweeping arc, instead of the desired tight turn. By controlling the edging with the knee, carefully bending it at an inward angle, you are actually setting your ski as you step, just right for the condition of the snow and the steepness of the terrain, while allowing it to take the full weight of your body. If you do not properly bend your right knee during this left turn, your weight will automatically shift to your left, or inside, ski and you will not be able to turn without having the skis cross each other. While you are bending your knees the skis will be less resistant to turning on the snow, and this is the proper time to be *Twisting*.

Twisting? Yes, it is somewhat like the twist. While you are *Kneeling*—bending your right knee at an angle and moving your weight forward—you lighten the pressure on your right ski. If you need proof try this at home on your bathroom scale: stand erect on the scale and look at the weight indicator; quickly drop your body, bending at the knees. The indicator will show that you weigh less as you drop. When you reach the lowest point of the drop the indicator will show your original weight. This little experiment should make clear that it is easier to twist your skis in a new direction while you are in the process of bending your knees.

These two actions, *Kneeling* and *Twisting*, must be combined so that they are one smooth motion. Practice putting them together while skiing in a Snowplow: as the knee bends, pivot the foot. Try a turn to the left—stop; now a turn to the right—stop. Next try linking the turns together, making an S curve. Don't keep your skis too far apart and don't turn too far in either direction. Stay close to the fall line. Before *Stepping* be sure to *Face* the ski you are to step on. Don't flatten the ski you are stepping on. Hold the edge. Don't forget: flattening is a natural tendency which you must combat.

You might like to picture this motion as stepping on a lighted cigarette butt. As you are in the process of *Kneeling* forward and inward at an angle, you are to grind the butt into the snow with your ski as if putting it out. Start with your weight on your left foot and imagine that a cigarette is just under the ball of your right foot, just behind the big toe. As you gradually put pressure on the cigarette by bending your right knee forward from the ankle at a slight inward angle, you grind the butt into the snow, twisting your right foot so that the toe is pointed to the left—that is, pivoting your foot counterclockwise, as in a column left marching step.

While you are bending your knee and twisting your foot your entire upper body must move forward to keep up with the speed of the ski. The *Twisting* action of your foot forces the ski to skid around the corner, lightly scraping the surface of the snow with its edge. The skid is controlled by the bending of the knee at the necessary angle for the condition of the snow and the steepness of the slope. The bent knee also creates a slight but ever-increasing edge. This edge holds the weight which is being brought forward, yet it allows the ski to drift. The edge also gives bite, or purchase, and security throughout the turn.

The Edge created by the Off-center Kneebend, a result of Controlled Kneeling, and the Turning of the Ski, a result of Twisting the Foot—these give you Purchase With Direction and Security while crossing the fall line. These specifications are very important to your safety!

We did not mention the unweighted left ski while we examined the left turn. You probably have it pushed out in a Snowplow position. The action of the unweighted ski is comparable to the action of the unweighted foot in making a left-hand turn while walking. You may, in the beginning, want to keep your skis in a Snowplow position, but sooner than you think you'll want them parallel. It's closer to the natural walking position and more comfortable. Since there is no weight on the uphill ski, at the completion of the left turn, simply bring it together with the downhill ski. As you twist the weighted downhill foot in the new direction move the unweighted uphill ski slightly forward, not a full stride ahead as in walking, but only about four inches. It is not necessary to move it forward any farther. For while skiing on an incline you are already in motion. You move the inside, unweighted ski ahead only in order to prevent it from crossing over the other ski during the turn—which would happen if you accidentally put any weight on it. This shift forward also helps to keep your weight on the proper leg; and further, in this position you can keep your knees closer together. Keeping the knees pressed together during the turn will act as a sturdy supporting post for maintaining balance and affords increased steering leverage for guiding the skis. In heavy snow, or in changing snow conditions, it is essential to keep the knees pressed together during turns; otherwise the skis will tend to go off in different directions.

Your upper body (shoulders, chest, hips) should also be used to help you turn your skis. As you turn a corner to the left while walking, you pivot on your right foot. As you twist your foot counterclockwise, your shoulders and hips turn involuntarily in the opposite direction. This action is commonly called "counterrotation." Try this simple experiment: Stand on a piano stool or stand on a small scatter rug. Twist your feet. You will find that your upper body will naturally twist in the opposite direction. The fifth key action, *Twisting,* uses the natural reaction of the upper body to the twist of the foot (*Facing* the ski you are about to step on).

If you combine all five actions in their proper order you will be able to make a natural and comfortable turn. Each action does its share to enable you to make a smooth turn, and at the end of each turn you should be *Facing* downhill so that you can see where you are going. Practice these turns on a slight grade in a partial Snowplow position, as close to the fall line as you can comfortably manage. Gradually rid yourself of the Snowplow position by bringing your skis closer and closer together. Occasionally as you are turning a corner, gently lift up the heel of the uphill ski about half an inch to prove to yourself it is weightless. Eventually, after some practice, the uphill ski should be parallel with *and* four inches forward of the downhill ski. If, when you try to raise the heel of the uphill ski, the entire ski comes up, your weight is too far back. If your weight is correctly forward, it will not be easy to raise the tip of the uphill ski. Keeping the uphill ski unweighted but gently pressed on the snow will give you added balance.

TRAVERSE

LESSON 3

We have already discussed the traverse position for climbing a hill. The following traverse is the position you use for going down and across a hill.

1. Start in the Running Position. (*Posture*) Put all your weight on your downhill ski, having it edged enough, naturally, to hold your weight. Place the uphill ski parallel to, but four inches in advance of, the downhill ski.

Fig. 64 Traverse position: Aimed only slightly downhill, you are in the Running position with your skis parallel, with uphill ski advanced four inches and all your weight on the edged downhill ski.

2. Stand on the side of the hill, skis edged and aimed slightly downhill. (Fig. 64) Keep yourself in position by putting your poles in front of you. Lift your poles. You will start to move down and across the fall line (steepest part of the slope) at a slight angle.

3. From this position go into a turn; you should now be facing in the opposite direction. Traverse the hill (cross the fall line) once more and turn again.

While in this traverse position practice using your edges to see what effect they have on the movement of the skis.

SIDESLIPPING

LESSON 4

All skiing turns involve sideslipping. Only by controlling your sideslipping will you be able to slow down or stop. You will recognize that even the Snowplow is a form of sideslipping except that the skis are aimed at each other instead of being parallel.

1. On the side of a hill get into a traverse position with your weight on your downhill ski. Bend your knees forward and into the hill to create an edge on which to ride. Your upper body should be facing the downhill ski.
2. Glide slowly across the hill with your knees together and your skis together. If all your weight is on your downhill ski, and none on your uphill ski, the skis will tend to stay together.
3. Slowly and gently swing your knees, as a unit, away from the hill. This will reduce the grip of your edges and flatten your skis, and you will begin to drift down the hill, sideways. (Fig. 65)
4. To slow down: While you are still drifting gently, swing your knees as a unit back toward the hill, subtly re-edging the skis. You will find yourself gradually scraping more snow beneath the running surface, thus slowing yourself down.
5. Try this sideslipping in both directions. Find some bumps on the slope, and practice sliding down the downhill side of the bumps. After you've practiced this for a while you should be able to do it on some fairly steep pitches.

If you have trouble starting to sideslip, try this:

Get yourself in a traverse position, facing downhill, with your skis aimed across a fairly steep grade. Place the spikes of your poles into the snow against the hill behind you, one on each side of you. (Fig. 66) Gently push yourself down the hill sideways, adjusting your edges with your knees to allow the skis to slip at a continuous and steady pace. A sensitive reduction of the edge grip will accomplish this. You will find that with the helpful pushing of your poles against the hill, you can drift at a steady

Fig. 65 Sideslip: From a Traverse position, slowly swing your knees away from the hill, flattening your skis, and drifting down the hill, sideways.

Fig. 66   If you have trouble
starting to Sideslip, push
yourself with your poles.

and controlled speed. Soon you will be able to do it without the help of poles.

You must be able to sideslip to get safely down very steep or unfamiliar terrain. The finesse with which you edge your skis is the chief indicator of your ability; it is also the key to relaxed, beautiful and pleasurable skiing.

The practice of sideslipping cannot be emphasized too much. Practice it in conjunction with small turns into the hill (uphill turns) and with your composite turn, the kneeling twist.

Remember, you only ski on *one* ski at a time—the downhill ski—and in spite of what some beginners think, there is only one downhill ski. It may be easier for you to keep the heel of your uphill ski about one inch off the snow in the beginning, proving to yourself that you are really skiing on the downhill ski only. Later, when you are more skilled at this, you'll know just where your weight is all the time.

SNOWPLOW CHRISTIANIA

LESSON 5

To do a Snowplow Christie, start down the hill in a partial (narrow) Snowplow. (Fig. 67) Gradually put your weight forward onto the downhill ski. (Fig. 68) Make the turn while holding it edged and allowing the uphill ski to flatten. The skis will come together in a parallel position. (Fig. 69)

Practice Snowplow Christies from the fall line into the hill in each direction, stopping at the completion of each one. Gradually do them closer and closer to the fall line. You'll find the skis getting closer and closer together. See! You're beginning to make parallel turns. Practice these small turns. Do them on both sides of the hill and on a little steeper terrain until they become smooth and steady.

Fig. 67 Start downhill in a partial (narrow) snowplow.

Fig. 68 Gradually put your weight forward on your downhill ski.

Fig. 69   Make a turn, holding the downhill ski edged and allowing the uphill ski to flatten. Your skis will come together.

HOW TO USE THE T-BAR

LESSON 6

Do not use a T-Bar, chairlift, or any other uphill facility until you can Snowplow and make a Snowplow Stop.

To get on:

1. Have your ticket ready and visible.
2. If you are going up on the right-hand side of the "T," take

Fig. 70   T-Bar position: Lean back slightly, but do NOT sit. Let the
T-Bar push you.

your poles off your wrist and hold them in your right hand (in your left hand if you are going up the left-hand side).

3. When your turn comes, move out fast so the lift crew can help you get on the T-Bar.

4. If you are going *up the right-hand* side, aim your skis up the hill slightly apart, knees slightly bent, not stiff. Turn your head, look over your left shoulder at the T-Bar as it comes toward you. When it reaches you, take the bar of the "T" with your left hand, and help ease the "T" part of the bar up to your seat. *Do not sit on it.* Stand up, lean slightly back and let it push you. (Fig. 70) Again, *do not sit!*

5. Steer your skis with your toes. There will be three tracks in the snow in front of you. Your left ski and your partner's right ski will be running in the center track side by side. Your right ski will be in the right track, his left ski in the far left track.

6. Put your right hand (which is still holding your poles) on the end of the "T." This will help steady you.

7. *To get off:* At the top of the hill, before you reach the getting-off place (there will be signs), pull yourself forward with your left hand, which is still gripping the bar, so that the "T" is not touching your seat. Gently push the "T" off to your left, and steer your skis to the right and out of the way of the people behind you.

The first time you ride the T-Bar, it is well to do it with an experienced, sympathetic skier.

Part Three

INTERMEDIATE TO ADVANCED

CHAPTER V

Advanced Turns

PARALLEL TURNS TO THE LEFT FROM A TRAVERSE POSITION

LESSON 1

Try a complete left turn from a traverse position and be conscious of the action of the separate parts of the body during every phase of the turn:

1. *Posture.* Get into a traverse position, skis together, and ski to your right diagonally across the hill. (Fig. 71) Check the following:

    a. All your weight on your left (downhill) ski.

    b. Right (uphill) ski advanced four inches.

    c. Downhill ski edged to hold you on your course, so that it is not slipping.

    d. Plan to step on your right foot, since you are now on your left foot.

2. In order to step on to your right foot, you must now start *Facing* your shoulders and hips slightly to the right so your chest will be aiming in the direction you are going to step.

3. Lead with your head as though you were diving; aim your head diagonally forward toward the tip of the uphill (right) ski. (Fig. 72) Use the left ski as a launching platform or springboard. Push your weight forward and off the left foot. *Step* toward, over and on to the right foot.

4. Your right knee should be bending to receive the weight of your entire body. (*Kneeling*) and turning in (downhill) to create a slight edge. This increasing edge forces the ski to bite the snow while allowing the ski to drift a bit, thus enabling you

Fig. 71 Traverse position, aimed diagonally across the hill to your right.

Fig. 72   Face the right, leading with your head.

to *Twist*. The bending and slightly in-turned knee will force your foot to *Twist* counterclockwise—steering and skidding the ski across the fall line toward the left. (Figs. 73 and 74) *Twisting* while you are bending the knee is easier, as we demonstrated before on the bathroom scale.

5. When you feel your right (now downhill) ski edge gradually gripping the snow, you will know your weight is properly

Fig. 73   LEFT. *Stepping* and *Kneeling:* Step onto the ball of the right foot, while bending the knee forward and inward.

Fig. 74   RIGHT. *Twist* your right foot counterclockwise, steering and skidding across the fall line to your left.

balanced over the ball of the right foot, directly behind the big toe, which is where it should be. Quickly bring the left, un-weighted (now uphill) ski parallel with the right ski and forward four inches. (Fig. 75) Advancing the ski four inches helps break the trail and leads the right ski around the turn.

Fig. 75   As your right ski edges into the snow, bring your unweighted left ski up parallel to the right one and four inches forward.

Caution: During the turn do not let your head wander from its correct position (out and over the outside, downhill ski—the right ski). Your hips and shoulders should also keep *Facing* the right ski throughout the turn. If you allow your head or your hips and shoulders to wander from their correct positions, the chances are that you are banking on the inside and will shift your weight to the left foot. If you make this weight shift during the turn, you will probably trip and fall. This weight shift is a common fault of the beginner. To combat it, learn to ski on one ski during the entire execution of every turn. After you become really skilled at turning, you may then equalize your weight or even bank on the inside at your discretion.

6. Your upper body should be *Facing* to the right in order to help you aim in the direction you are *Stepping*. You may continue to turn your torso more to the right as you turn your skis to the left, if you make sure to keep your back straight—which is the correct position in any case. This makes the ski easier to turn. It is called the comma position. It is as though you were attempting to sit in an imaginary chair, with your torso facing straight downhill while your knees aim across the slope to your left. This extreme position is much used on steep terrain to get a better bite, or grip, with the ski's edges.

AN ABRUPT STOP DURING A PARALLEL TURN

LESSON 2

If you quickly counterrotate your shoulders and hips, turning them in the opposite direction from which the skis are going while leaning out, you force your body into a sharp comma position, especially if the knees are bent forward and in at an angle —which is their correct position. This whirling out of the upper body will cause the skis to edge deeply, and stop fast.

GARLANDS

LESSON 3

Garlands are a series of short parallel turns into the slope made from a traverse. They leave a pattern in the snow which resembles garlands. You must practice making Garlands in order to improve the coordination between the bend of your knee and the twist of your foot: *Facing* and *Twisting* in opposite directions.

After you make this quick turn into the hill to your left, poke the spike of your pole hard into the snow to the left of your left ski and push off from it. This will start you down the hill again, and when you have gained enough speed, make another parallel turn to the left, into the hill.

Practice making Garlands across the hill many times both to the left and to the right. Start with a nearly lateral series and gradually move closer and closer to the fall line. In an actual full turn (approximately 360 degrees) this garland exercise is really the last part of the maneuver, minus the crossing of the fall line.

TURNING ON ONE SKI

LESSON 4

If you can balance yourself on one foot, you should be able to turn that foot while moving slowly and stay balanced; therefore you should be able to ski with your skis held tightly together at all times (parallel). You can do this without going too fast by using a slight up-and-down motion. Here's how:

1. Stand on a mild slope, skis aimed downhill; hold yourself in this position by placing your poles in the snow in front of you.

2. First think about your *Posture*, then put all your weight on your right ski.

3. Ease up on your poles and allow your skis to move ahead slightly. As the skis start to move, quickly perform the other four actions in order: *Face, Step, Kneel, Twist*. The right ski should turn to the left smoothly.

How to keep your skis together while turning a sharp corner from a standing position:

1. Select a bump; stand on it with your ski pointing left in a traverse position.

2. Perform the five actions in order: *Posture, Face, Step, Kneel* and *Twist*.

3. The up-and-down motion is simply the stepping motion or the transferring of weight from the right to the left foot. *Step* up on the uphill ski before beginning the turn. The down motion is simply the *Kneeling* action or kneeling into the left or turning ski.

4. The ski will turn and the skis will stay together if you consciously force them to. Think them together. If they do separate it's probably because you haven't been keeping boot against boot throughout the turn.

PRACTICE

LESSON 5

Practice your parallel turns from a traverse position on a fairly mild slope. In the beginning, do not link them together. After you have mastered them singly begin to link them together, but keep a long traverse so you will have time to think about what you're going to do next.

Gradually bring your turns more and more into the fall line. Eventually you should be making short little turns back and forth across the fall line. You do not complete each turn; if you did you would take yourself out of the fall line and lose the continuous flowing motion you want. The end of one turn is the beginning of the next. You can see how it resembles walking downhill.

By using your poles as you do this you will get a more precise balance each time you shift your weight from one foot to the other.

HOW TO USE YOUR POLES

LESSON 6

If you have managed to turn without the use of your poles it is obvious that you are skiing well and your balance is excellent. Beginning and intermediate skiers very often rely too much on their poles and are sometimes unable to tell whether it is their poles that are turning them or their skiing skill.

Before we discuss the use of poles let's review what we said about the use and position of the arms while walking. As the left foot goes forward, the right arm swings forward; as the right foot goes forward, the left arm swings forward. This is also true in skiing. The left hand goes forward when the right foot goes forward, and the spike of the left-hand pole is placed in the snow in line with, but not ahead of, the right boot.

When turning, the point of the pole is placed a little ahead of where you would place it while walking on skis to give you time to use it and quickly bring it back out of the way. Try it making a left-hand turn:

1. Hold your poles with your thumbs on top of the handle grips. Traverse across the slope to your right—weight on the downhill ski, body facing downhill, skis together.

2. With your elbows close at your sides move your left hand, wrist, and forearm out to your left, and swing the spike of the left pole ahead, as you might a cane. For a left turn the left pole is put beside the left ski.

3. Push off, quickly taking the pole out of the snow. Pushing the pole in the snow in this manner has helped you balance yourself on the ball of the right foot (the *Twisting* point). The push you get from the pole moves you toward your other ski. The two motions: putting the pole in the snow and springing from the inside edge of the left ski, give smoothness, and eventually beauty, to the turn.

You can see now how helpful the poles are in deep snow or in difficult snow conditions. They act as a lifting tool. We would call these small jump turns if the heels of the skis were actually lifted off the snow while using the poles.

WEDELN

LESSON 7

Wedeln means "fishtailing." If you practice quick parallel turns using your poles correctly and keeping your skis almost flat, you will find yourself wedelning. Your chest should remain facing downhill; the heels of your skis will shift from side to side. "Fishtailing" is what it looks like from the rear: the slightly edged skis zigzagging as they lightly brush the surface of the snow going down the hill.

Wedeln seems to be the ultimate in skiing performance at present, for it requires excellent timing to use a pole at the exact instant the other foot is stepped upon. The controlled knee creates just the right amount of edge to be applied for the snow conditions and slope steepness. The amount and speed with which the foot *Twists* helps determine the amount of sharpness of the curve.

SKATING AND SKATING TURNS

LESSON 8

Skating on skis is a great exercise to improve your ability to balance yourself on one ski; it also gives you a clearer picture of what, in a general way, skiing is all about. Instead of continually thinking about the many details involved, try occasionally to think of skiing in a broader way: skiing, after all, is merely skating down a hill one foot at a time while balancing yourself in an upright position. Thinking about skiing in this way may improve your form.

Correct skating on skis is a marvelous blend of coordinated body motion which produces a slow and easily controlled glide. You will not be able to skate on skis unless your body is forward and directly over one ski, which should be slightly edged. The edge is, of course, created by the controlled knee bend.

SKIING MOGULS

LESSON 9

Skiers usually make their turns on the slopes and trails in about the same spot. This causes the snow from their skidding to pile up and form bumps which are called moguls. Bumps or moguls can be very upsetting for the skier used to skiing a bumpless practice slope. If you don't want to go sailing into the air from mogul to mogul, picking up speed as you go, you had better try the following.

1. As you approach a mogul you want to ride over, try to keep your body straight; that is, allow your knees and skis to be drawn up under you as the crown of the mogul pushes them up, but keep your back straight. In other words, don't fight the bump, cooperate with it. When you get to the hollow, on the other side of the mogul, let your legs straighten out. This is similar to the action of a car: when your car hits a bump the

wheels give to absorb the shock, but the chassis (your torso) remains stationary.

2. If you are going fast turn your skis sideways on the crest of the mogul and slide down in a parallel Christie position, gradually increasing your edges to slow you down.

3. You might enjoy moving along at a fast clip and picking your way through the little valleys and gullies that surround each mogul. This requires fast pole work plus *Stepping, Kneeling* and *Twisting* on each foot. Use your edges to slow yourself up on the downhill slope of each mogul.

4. Moguls are useful for learning to sideslip. Sliding down their downhill sides will improve your form.

5. Do not try to Snowplow over or between moguls; your skis will probably get crossed.

SKIING ON ICE

LESSON 10

In the east the slopes are often icy. Instead of being afraid of the ice, why not learn to ski on it and enjoy it?

1. Sharpen the steel edges of your skis with a file. Put the ski on its side with the running surface turned away from you; push the file in single strokes toward the running surface, across the thickness of the steel edge. This will put a sharp burr on the steel and give you a better grip on the ice.

2. Unless you can't avoid it, don't turn on the ice; ski across it and pick a patch of snow to turn on. As you cross the ice, ride on the downhill ski only. Your head should be out over the downhill ski. Bend your knees in at a sharp angle to create and hold a sharp edge.

3. If you have to turn on the ice, carefully apply as much edge as you possibly can to lessen the slipping and make sure that every bit of your weight is on the downhill ski.

4. Short, quick jump turns will give you a better grip on a long section of the ice.

5. Make yourself ski under icy conditions and learn how to adjust your skiing to them. You will conquer your fear and become a better skier. After you are accustomed to skiing on icy gentle slopes, try some steeper terrain under icy conditions.

DEEP-SNOW SKIING

LESSON 11

Skiing in deep snow (snow which has not been packed down or skied on) requires keen coordination between mind and muscle to make smooth turns.

1. Place your weight slightly further back on your heels than ordinarily. This will help you lift your toes against the roof of your boot, thus raising the tips of your skis to the surface of the snow. This is called "planing" the skis. If your weight were in its usual place, forward, the skis would drive deep into the snow, making it impossible to turn.

2. Your weight should be evenly distributed rather than on one foot at a time.

3. Use your poles to give you a more pronounced "up motion." This will make *Twisting* easier and enable you to turn.

4. Deliberately twist your body with more force in both directions. This also makes turning easier.

SKIING STEEP TERRAIN

LESSON 12

To be an expert skier you must know how to control your skis on steep slopes.

It is very easy to pick up speed. To avoid this you must keep the body over the pad of the foot so you have instantaneous control. The steeper the slope, the further forward you should be. Your natural instinct will be to hold yourself back, to hug the hill, but the safest position is perpendicular to the slope.

The shovel or curved part of the front of your ski is wider than any other part of it. If your weight is forward, this shovel presses firmly into the snow and slows the skis down because of its width. Make slight jump turns or hops, using your poles to help you unweight the heels of your skis. When lifted slightly, the skis can readily be made to move from side to side, allowing you to turn more easily. Be sure to increase your edge quickly by increasing the angle of your knee bend. Use a good elastic knee action, and bend from the ankle to catch the shock of the oncoming weight. A series of quick jump turns in conjunction with a quick, sharp reversal of the shoulders and hips in unison forces the skis to turn neatly with a slim chance of error. The poles should be placed in the snow for only an instant. As you jab the pole you should be *Facing, Stepping, Kneeling* and *Twisting* with the opposite foot. The quick jab of the pole gives you the final adjustment of balance counteracting the step on the opposite foot.

Part Four

SKIING TIPS

CHAPTER VI

Bad Habits and How to Get Rid of Them

BENDING AT THE WAIST

Do not bend from the waist. It is natural to want to get as close to the ground as possible so that you will have less distance to fall, but bending from the waist can be disastrous. It forces your seat back over your heels and puts your chest forward. This essentially awkward position increases your speed to the point where you are unable to control it. In addition, if you bend from the waist you will find it difficult to bend your knees and ankles and will thus lose control of the skis. Your body will behave like a seesaw, tottering over every bump. It is a very unstable position.

Stand erect, with your seat over the pad of the foot and your chest in line with your seat. Your knees should be slightly bent so that you are kneeling forward from the ankles. This is the Running Position, and it is constant. Practice this position while you are stopped on a slope, while waiting in the lift line or while waiting your turn in ski class. The Running Position (*Posture*) must become second nature if you are ever to become an expert skier.

WEIGHT TOO FAR BACK

Beginners usually fall backward when they hit their first bump because their weight is too far back and their skis slide out from under them.

If you just stand on your skis on a flat area you will see that because of the position of the bindings your weight is too far back to give you any control. Your entire body must roll forward from the ankles as it does when you walk or your skis will simply slip out from under you. This is particularly true in turning. There is a tendency for beginners to settle back on their heels when completing a turn. Combat this by practicing the *Posture* position and creating good habits.

LOOKING AT YOUR SKIS

Do not look at your skis. Looking at your skis forces you to bend from the waist and does not permit you to see what's ahead. Keep your eyes on the snow about twenty feet ahead of you. Even looking this far ahead, you will still be able to see your skis peripherally.

STRAIGHT LEGS

If you intend to balance yourself on skis on an incline or on uneven terrain, you must have springs or shock absorbers to help you. The *Kneeling* action of your knees, bending or straightening (but not straight), will absorb this unevenness.

While you are walking, the bent knee receives the weight of the body. This is also true when you shift the weight while skiing. The downhill knee must bend slightly to receive the oncoming weight. Practice *Kneeling* with the downhill knee during every turn; be sure the body is upright when you practice this. In addition to catching the weight, the controlled kneel creates the edge and makes it easier for the foot to *Twist* the ski in the desired direction.

LEANING THE BODY INTO THE HILL
DURING TURNS

This is a natural tendency (from riding a bicycle, etc.) which you must counteract. In order to be secure on skis, you must do exactly the opposite—lean away from the hill. If you do lean into the hill you will be putting an edge on the uphill ski and will cause it to cross the downhill ski. This is commonly called "catching an edge," and it usually causes a spill.

To prevent this common error here's what you can do:

a.) On every turn lead with your head and keep it directly over the outside ski throughout the turn. Do not "cut the corner" on the inside. Make sure you are turning your ski with your controlled *Kneel* and your foot *Twist*.

b.) Keep your body *Facing* the outside ski throughout the turn and never look back. Experience will perfect your timing. As long as your upper body is turning in the opposite direction from your skis, you will *not* "lean into the hill."

BRINGING THE SHOULDERS AND HIPS AROUND WITH THE TURN

This is called rotating. It can be eliminated by concentrating on the fact that the uphill shoulder *always* goes back before a turn—naturally, the hip with it—and *stays* there throughout the turn. Making Garlands is splendid practice for training the upper body to counterrotate as the knee bends and the feet twist. Remember the second action word, *Facing*, and practice it in the Snowplow turn enough times to form a habit.

If you still are having trouble, slow yourself down by getting on a mild snowplow and move slowly. Watch yourself as you say each of the five action words in succession and see to it that you make your body mind your commands. Do this over and over again. Decrease your snowplow position, allowing more speed as you can take it. Speed, of course, is last!

CHAPTER VII

How to Start Your Children Skiing

ANN DAY

How soon can we put our children on skis? Is my five-year-old boy too young to go to ski school? What ski equipment should I buy for my children? What should I do if my child gets discouraged?

As soon as your youngster can walk, he can be put on a pair of small, inexpensive skis. Let him play on level ground (at the bottom of the ski slope) until he becomes familiar with the skis. Show him how to walk on skis, and push him so the skis slide for a short distance; children love the feeling of gliding. Walk along beside him on your own skis, holding him by the hand. This will build his confidence. Don't expect his interest to last too long. Be ready to take off his skis as soon as you see he's not having fun. He will want to put them on again sooner than you think. Never leave a very small child alone on skis. Plan your day so that you can spend some time playing with him. Your child should feel from the beginning that skiing is only for fun and that it is something that the entire family can do together. Your child will not become discouraged if he is not pushed too hard.

At three or four years, he will learn to balance himself on skis and, when he feels at home on them, you can occasionally take him up on the T-Bar or Poma Lift between your legs. Bring him down a gentle slope in the same way. It is relatively easy to Snowplow down a slope with a three-year-old between your legs. (Fig. 76) Go slowly so your child will get a feeling of the Snowplow and the Snowplow turn. You should encourage him to put

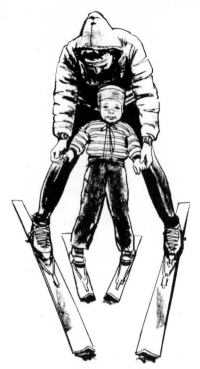

Fig. 76   Snowplow down a gentle slope, keeping your three- or four-year-old safely between your legs.

all his weight on his own skis and to bend his knees from the ankle. Do not lift or drag him.

At five or six, children can usually ski on their own down a relatively easy slope. They stay out in the snow longer and take a keen interest in improving their form. At this age they also like to play games. Set up an obstacle course around trees or ski poles or play follow-the-leader. Children tend to take the straightest course downhill; they should be encouraged to turn as much as possible; and for their own safety and the safety of others, they should be taught controlled speed.

At seven or eight, children like to imitate adults and will begin to turn in the manner of the parent or the instructor. They enjoy ski classes and progress rapidly. If encouraged they will abandon the Snowplow and quite easily learn parallel turns. Some children at this age, however, only like to play, and they should be encouraged since they will certainly learn as much from playing games on skis as they would in class. Don't push them into class until they show a real desire to improve their form. A short slalom course of ten or fifteen gates will keep a group of children happy all afternoon. It will make them think and learn to turn.

Children nine through twelve like lots of activity. Their minds are quick and they learn fast. They like to get off the beaten trail; they like to ski through the woods and around trees. As soon as they learn to ski in control, they should go up on a lift to a major trail with an adult. Make them follow you down the trail, keeping them behind you at all times. Make as many turns as possible. Give your child the incentive to improve. At this age they like games, obstacle courses and, above all, races. Almost every ski area has sponsored races for this age group. It is important to a ten- or twelve-year-old to show progress and measure it by his accomplishments. Mostly, they love speed, so be sure they have a certain grasp of the fundamentals before you allow them to attempt maneuvers beyond their abilities. The most important thing at this energetic, pre-teen-age is lots of skiing. Interest develops and skill improves with the amount of skiing.

Teen-age children should join adult classes. They have more patience and can follow the instructions. They will enjoy following the instructions in this book, especially if an adult in the family is learning too. Some children learn fast and have good balance and coordination; others ski awkwardly and are slow to learn. One of the joys of skiing is that fast or slow, awkward or graceful, there is pleasure in it for all. Teen-agers are not easily discouraged and enjoy going to ski class. There they meet other skiers their own age, compare their progress, encourage each other and, what is most important, have fun.

Do not rush your children, especially if you yourself are a good skier. Let them learn at their own speed. Be sure they learn all the basic essentials. Patience (yours) and enthusiasm are most important. Whatever the age of your child, be interested in his progress and his problems. Don't leave him to flounder by himself. Ski with him as much as possible.

If you begin to learn to ski at the same time as your child, of whatever age, he will very quickly be skiing better, and certainly faster, than you. Don't be discouraged; be philosophical. Encourage him, but don't compete; if you do compete you will certainly lose, and so will your child.

SKI SCHOOL

Do not put your child in ski school until he has been on skis a few times. Allow him to try out his skis by walking and playing around, climbing and gently gliding down a small incline. He should be accustomed to his skis and poles before being exposed to formal instruction. Unless he is a really unusual child (and what child isn't?) don't expect him to get much out of a two-hour ski class until he is eight or nine. However, many ski areas have special classes for children conducted by excellent instructors. These classes for small children will give your child the basic steps without burdening him with information; they are also fun. Many parents have difficulty teaching their own children to ski. Too much of "don't do this" and "don't do that" make it too much like home discipline. The result can be a disappointed and unhappy child. As a general rule, a stranger (ski instructor) is better. Encourage your child to practice what he has learned in class, and do it with him on his level, but don't insist. With a combination of good children's classes, encouragement and a certain amount of freedom, your child will be skiing better than you.

EQUIPMENT

At four years or younger, a child can begin with small wooden skis, wooden poles and just a toe strap. Use overshoes and rubber bands to keep the skis on. We bought boots and bindings for our children when they were five years old, but they used the same wooden skis. With good boots and safety bindings, they progressed rapidly.

The next things to buy are skis with steel edges. They will need steel edges as soon as they are ready for sideslipping and Christies. Don't buy skis that are too long for the child. The ski shop will help you find the proper size, but they should not come above the child's wrist when stood on end. The poles should be about chest high. Because children's boots are made of less expensive leather than adults (and happily they *are* less expensive) it is important to keep them in a boot press at all times. Your child will get more wear out of them if the soles are kept flat. Dress your child warmly; he will be easily discouraged if he is cold. It's not necessary to buy expensive equipment and clothing until you are sure your child likes to ski. Most ski areas rent equipment for children by the day or week.

GAMES

Children get bored climbing up and sliding down a small incline. Here are a few games that will hold their interest, improve their balance and teach them to turn:

Under the Bridges

Set up a pair of ski poles in the snow about three or four feet apart near the bottom of a hill. Put the ends of a third pole through the hoops of the standing poles, making a bridge. They ski under the bridge by bending their knees and assuming a squatting position. It's best if they do not use their poles during this game. Encourage them to squat low enough to hold their knees. This teaches them balance and strengthens their legs, especially their thighs. You can make a series of these bridges of different heights by using poles of varying lengths. (Fig. 77)

Ski-Pole Stop

Using ski poles set up a series of gates in a straight course down a gentle slope. Have the children start at the top of the hill and come down in a controlled Snowplow through each gate. As they reach each gate they must do a Snowplow Stop, count to five and then go on to the next gate, until they have gone through each gate and reached the bottom of the hill.

Obstacle Course

Set up an easy course by using the bridges, Snowplow Stop gates, and other slalom combinations. Make it easy to start with, and add more obstacles as their skill increases.

Fig. 77 Children can ski under ski-pole bridges, squatting low enough to hold their knees.

Fox and Hounds

Lay out a course in the snow and have the children chase each other around the paths or through the woods. They can also play tag on this course. Put a bright hat on one of the faster skiers and see who can retrieve it.

Follow the Leader

First lead the children around the slope and through the woods; then let them take turns being the leader. You can also take children on a cross-country tour. They like making fresh tracks in the snow.

These stunts and games are for the obvious purpose of building up the child's confidence, improving his balance and sharpening his coordination. These games will also help him with the basic maneuvers. Before you know it your child will be skiing the expert trails; let's hope you'll be skiing them with him.

CHAPTER VIII

Questions and Answers

Here are the questions most often asked in ski school; I hope I have been able to anticipate some of yours.

I use the rotation method to turn; why is there no mention of it in your book?

I did not want to confuse those beginners who are using this book with conflicting techniques. If you use the rotation method to turn and it works for you, continue to use it, by all means. However, I think counterrotation is more logical, safer and gives you more security. Your knees and your feet are your steering apparatus, and they actually make your skis turn no matter what your upper body is doing. I have found over the years that counterrotation, which conforms to the laws of physics ("every action produces an opposite and equal reaction"), produces a smoother turn. If you use rotation, you run the danger of "over-swinging" or "overrotating," whereas in counterrotation you eliminate the unnecessary motion of carrying your shoulders and hips around the corner with your skis. A further advantage of counterrotation: at the end of each turn you are facing downhill and can see where you're going next.

Why haven't you shown us how to do a Stem-Turn or a Stem-Christiania?

Stem-turns and Stem-Christianias are transitional exercises formerly used to get the beginning skier from Snowplowing to parallel skiing. If you learn to Snowplow properly, meanwhile strengthening your foot muscles and improving your balance, by using the walking movements we have discussed you can move right into parallel skiing without learning to stem at all.

Why do my skis cross when I do a Snowplow?
Your skis will tend to cross if you:
1. Bend at the waist.
2. Edge your skis too much.
3. Do not keep your ski tips apart by using the front of your foot.

How can I keep my skis together all the time?
You must be able to ski completely on one ski and be able to turn on one ski (Chapter V, Lesson 4). You will find it a matter of concentrating on keeping your boots and knees together.

What can I do to avoid getting hurt skiing?
1. Buy good equipment.
2. Adjust your safety bindings properly.
3. Stay in good physical condition.
4. Know how to turn and slow down in any and all circumstances.
5. Be alert to all possible dangers on the slope—ahead and to the sides.
6. Ski with reasonable speed.
7. Rest frequently: do not work yourself to the point of sudden, unexpected exhaustion.
8. Practice on easy terrain. Improve your skiing skills constantly until you are free from fear and feel at home. Only then venture onto steeper slopes and—last of all—gain speed.

How long will it take me to learn how to ski?
As long as it takes you to strengthen your foot muscles, balance yourself securely and turn your skis.

How can I keep from getting cold while skiing?
Fingers and toes get cold first and then, in cold high winds, your nose and ears. Wear mittens, not gloves, large enough to allow the warm air from your hands to circulate around your fingers. Wool socks are better than cotton; wool holds warm air and allows your body moisture to escape. To protect your face from freezing in high winds, wear a face mask or carry a large

pocket handkerchief and tie it around your face under the eyes. Always ski with someone anyway, but especially on bitter cold days when there is danger of frostbite. In the first stages, patches of skin become grayish white. Cover the affected area.

I am just a beginner, but my friends who are experienced skiers want me to go to the top of the mountain with them. They say it's safe. Should I go?

No. The unknowing beginner wants to be a good sport and go along with his friends, possibly thinking to himself, "Well, if they can do it, so can I." He does not realize the tremendous speeds he can quickly attain at such heights. Not being really skilled in stopping or even in slowing down, the poor novice gets more of a fright from helplessness than he or his friends imagined. This fright may be enough to make him quit skiing for good; or he might skid off the trail into the woods where he can hurt himself badly.

Learn well, and have fun skiing with your more advanced friends *only when you really can control your skis.*

Does skiing have to be expensive?

No. The initial cost of your equipment is fairly high (what sporting equipment isn't?) but if you take good care of it, it should last you a long time. Children, of course, outgrow their things quickly, but skiing families are always happy to make an equitable trade.

Most ski areas have package plans which include lodging, ski lifts, rental of equipment and ski instruction at substantial savings. Staying at local farmhouses can greatly reduce the cost of a ski weekend.

Skis, poles, boots, bindings and warm clothing are all that is absolutely necessary for skiing. All ski shops have end-of-season sales, when you can pick up equipment and clothing at ridiculously low prices.

Cross-country skiing costs relatively little. It's a splendid and leisurely way of seeing the countryside; it is challenging and is one of the most satisfying kinds of skiing.

Why do so many people want to ski?

First of all, it's a wonderful way to enjoy what might otherwise be a miserable, cold and unpleasant winter. The sun, air and heavy snowstorms are all invigorating and revitalizing. It's also fun! There is an enormous satisfaction to be had from coordinating the mind and the muscles of the body and controlling the skis down steep and difficult terrain. Each skier is entirely on his own; each must realize his own limitations and work hard at overcoming them. There is an endless challenge in learning more and more control, in going faster and faster down more and more difficult trails. And it's one of the few sports that any number can join in. It's great fun for the whole family to ski together—from toddlers to grandparents—or you can go alone with a friend.

A Short Note on the History of Skiing

Skiing began in the Scandinavian countries and northern Siberia. Skis were originally used for transporting heavy loads over long distances on ice and snow. Skis date back to about 2000 B.C. They probably developed from the walking snowshoe.

The principal technique used for turning skis before 1890 originated in Telemark, Norway. The Telemark turn is not used very much today because we have different bindings. To turn left, in those days, the skier moved his right ski far forward, extended his arms to the sides, brought his left ski up, tip touching the instep of the right foot, and levered himself around. This turn and the Open Christiania (ski slightly separated in the front) were the only turns used. In Austria, in 1869 a man named Zdarsky, who was probably the first professional ski instructor, published a book called *Alpine Ski Technique*. By 1904 he had taught over a thousand people to ski. He is also remembered for his improvement of the M2 Norwegian harness or foot binding. He rigged the heel to prevent the sideways play of the foot.

Hannes Schneider, the developer of the Schneider or Austrian Technique, got his first training at the age of fourteen from Victor Schimel, an adherent of the pure Norwegian style. In 1907 Schneider started his professional career as a ski instructor at St. Anton-am-Alberg in the Tyrol. No skiing theory existed at this time. The pupil simply imitated the instructor. Schneider found as he schussed the alpine meadows that if he bent his knees, thereby lowering his center of gravity, he could keep his balance and not fall so frequently. By putting more weight on one ski Schneider found a method of controlling speed that is still used today.

Schneider's method consisted of learning the Snowplow, Snowplow turn, Stem-turn, Stem-Christiania and Parallel Swing. It also consisted of "rotation," that is, rotating the body in the direction of the turn.

The Tyrolean Professional Ski Teachers, founded in 1925, and the German Ski Association adopted the Schneider method, and it was taught throughout the Tyrol. Two movies of Schneider in action demonstrating his complete control were shown throughout Europe and aroused great interest in the sport. Schneider also trained soldiers during World War I to ski with rifles and packs on their backs. His fame spread, and people flocked to the Tyrol to ski.

Skiing began in the United States about 1860. It was brought to this country by the Norwegians who settled around the Great Lakes. These Scandinavians showed the pioneers who were going west how to cover vast distances during the winter by using skis. Skiing as a sport started about 1900. The Ishpeming Ski Club, founded in Ishpeming, Michigan in 1887, was the first ski club in America. Soon others started, supported by the Scandinavians who had settled in Wisconsin, Minnesota and Upper Michigan.

Ski jumping was the big attraction, and ski clubs which held jumps created great interest. The National Ski Association of America was founded in Ishpeming, Michigan in 1904.

The founding of the Dartmouth Outing Club by Fred Harris in 1910, and its annual winter carnival, brought skiing to the attention of the country.

Dartmouth and its graduates have had a strong influence on American skiing. The school has always been sensitive to new theories and practices from abroad, and they have had such distinguished coaches as Colonel Anton Diettrich and Otto Schneibs from Germany and Walter Prager from Switzerland. Otto Schneibs, because of his sound teaching methods and enthusiastic love of the sport, has probably done more than any other man in the United States to promote skiing.

During the 1920's skiing consisted mostly of jumping and college competitions. The first downhill slalom race was held in 1927 on Mt. Moosilauke Carriage Road at the suggestion of Colonel Diettrich of Dartmouth. Prior to the 1920's ski jumping in America was based on the Norwegian jumping and cross-country technique (body erect). About this time the Schneider method from Central Europe was introduced. The first American ski school was probably Pecketts-On-Sugar-Hill in Franconia, New Hampshire. It was opened in 1931 by Sig Buchmayr.

In 1932 the United States played host to the Winter Olympics, and this event really sparked recreational skiing in this country. In 1933 the CCC built many ski trails and shelters which helped move the sport along. The first rope tow was started in Woodstock, Vermont by Bunny Bertrand. Others quickly sprang up.

When Hitler marched into Austria, the Hannes Schneider ski school was broken up. Many of his instructors escaped to France and Switzerland, but Schneider himself was put in prison. Through the influence of Harvey Gibson of North Conway, New Hampshire, Schneider was released and brought to this country with his children to establish his famous ski school.

Roland Palmedo, an enthusiastic ski booster and a committee chairman in the Eastern Ski Association, began a movement in the 1930's to raise the level of, and to standardize, ski instruction. This brought about the Certification System of the Eastern Ski Association, which certifies qualified ski instructors.

Recreational skiing was interrupted during the war, but many great skiers and ski instructors came out of the 10th Mountain Division, which was trained for combat skiing.

In 1948 Emile Allais, fresh from his triumph as a racer in international competition, toured the United States and caused a brief flurry of interest in his French technique. His technique consisted of gathering speed before a turn, then just before making the turn rolling forward onto the tips of the skis while rotating the body in the direction of the turn and contracting the stomach muscles to lift the heels off the snow.into what he called a "ruade" position. With the heels off the snow the skis could then be easily twisted in the desired direction. The method was tried and had a brief rage, but it was too difficult for the average skier.

More racing on an international scale and an increased interest in the fastest way to get through slalom flags produced some startling results. The first was Anton Seelos's discovery that by reversing the body rotation during a turn, the turn became easier to make. It was a startling discovery that has changed skiing. The reverse shoulder technique has been used with great success in all national and international competitions since 1940. The Austrian ski schools now use reverse shoulder and call it the Modified Alberg Ski Technique. It certainly is easier, more logical and more efficient in getting to the bottom of the hill.

GLOSSARY

ADVANCED. Skiers who are able to make parallel turns.

ALBERG STRAP. A leather strap fastened to the bindings for additional ankle support. It also prevents skis from "running away" when the safety bindings are released.

BASKET. The part of the ski pole which prevents the spikes from going too deeply into the snow.

BEGINNER. A skier who has not mastered the Snowplow or Snowplow Stop.

BEND. To kneel from the ankle, bringing the chest and seat forward as a unit.

BINDING. A metal device which keeps the boot fastened to the ski.

BITE OR GRIP. The purchase or hold a ski has on the side of a hill.

BOTTOMS. The running surface of skis.

CHAIR LIFT. A single or double chair suspended from a cable which carries one or two people to the top of a mountain.

CHRISTIANIA. A skid or sideslip made while in a parallel position.

COMMA POSITION. Head and shoulders twisted facing and over the downhill ski; hip on the uphill side of the uphill ski.

CROSS-COUNTRY TOURING. A trip on skis over gentle terrain and rolling hills.

DOWNHILL SKI. The ski closest to the bottom of the hill.

DRIFT. Another word for sideslipping.

EDGE. The outside or inside rim of a ski's running surface.

EDGING TIPPING. To tip the ski into the snow using the knee or ankle or both.

EXPERT. A skier whose speed is always under control and who can handle any type of terrain, however difficult, under any snow or ice conditions.

FACING. The second key action. Turning or twisting your shoulders and hips (as a unit) in the direction toward which you are going to shift your weight.

FALL LINE. A hill's steepest line of descent.

FLATTENING SKIS. Putting the entire running surface of the ski on the snow.

GRADE. The pitch or angle of a slope.

HEEL OF THE SKI. The tail or back end of the ski.

HERRINGBONE. A method of climbing on skis with the tips of the skis widely separated and the heels of the skis close together.

INTERMEDIATE. A skier who can ski almost any trail but who is not secure and comfortable when making parallel turns.

JUMP TURN. A move in a new direction made by lifting the heels of the skis (or the entire skis) off the snow.

KICK TURN. A 180° turn made usually on level ground, moving one ski at a time.

KNEELING. The fourth key action. Bending the knee at a slight angle to receive the oncoming weight and create an edge.

LOOP. The leather circular strap at the top of the ski pole through which you put your hand to prevent it from sliding down the shaft of the pole.

NOVICE. A skier who has mastered the Snowplow and the Snowplow Stop.

PARALLEL. Skis together.

127

PARALLEL CHRISTIANIA. A sideslipping turn executed with the skis together.

PIVOTING. Twisting the ski in a new direction by turning the ball of the foot.

POSTURE. The first key action word. It is also called the Running Position: upper body erect; knees slightly bent; upper body directly over the balls of the feet; all the body's weight on the pads of the feet; body leaning forward at a slight angle.

RUNNING POSITION. See *Posture.*

RUNNING SURFACE. The bottom of the ski.

SAFETY BINDING. A mechanism which releases the foot from the ski automatically under pressure.

SAFETY CLIPS. Small leather straps with a clip on each end. Used to keep the ski attached loosely to the boot in case the safety binding should release.

SCHUSS. To ski straight down a hill without turning.

SHAFT. The tubular or straight section of the ski pole.

SIDESLIP. To slide down the slope sideways, scraping snow slightly with your edges.

SIDESTEP. A method of climbing sideways; skis parallel, using the uphill edge of each ski to get a grip on the snow.

SKATING. Skiing on one ski at a time. A pleasurable exercise for improving your balance, for learning to ski on one ski and for learning to keep your weight forward.

SKI TIP. The front or pointed end of the ski.

SLIP. Sideslip.

SNOWPLOW. To ski with your skis in an inverted "V," tips close, heels apart. A maneuver used to control speed, especially for beginners. Useful for learning muscular coordination and edge control.

SNOWPLOW CHRISTIE. A turn which begins in the Snowplow position and ends with the skis parallel.

SPIKES. The sharp ends of the ski poles.

STARTING POSITION. The Running Position or Posture, but with the poles in the snow.

STEEL EDGES. The outside and inside rims of the running surface of the ski.

STEM-CHRISTIANIA. A transition exercise used to bridge the gap between Snowplow and parallel skiing, unnecessary in this method.

STEPPING. The third key action. The forward diagonal motion of the body moving as a unit to shift the weight to the opposite ski.

SWIVEL (BINDING). The adjustable front toe piece of the safety binding, which shifts positions, thus releasing the boot if a heavy lateral strain is put on it.

T-BAR. A mechanical device which will take you to the top of the mountain standing up.

TRAVERSE. To go up or down a slope diagonally.

TWISTING. The fifth key action. The pivoting of the foot which turns the ski as the body counterrotates.

UPHILL SKI. The ski furthest from the base of the hill.

WEDELN. To make quick parallel turns, keeping skis almost flat; to "fishtail."

WEIGHT. In skiing, the chest and hips.

WEIGHTING. Moving the chest and hips as a unit.